5/97

Capstone Short Biographies

Hispanic Scientists

Ellen Ochoa, Carlos A. Ramírez, Eloy Rodriguez, Lydia Villa-Komaroff, Maria Elena Zavala

by Jetty St. John

CAPSTONE PRESS

MANKATO

C A P S T O N E   P R E S S
818 North Willow Street • Mankato, MN 56001

Printed in the United States of America.

Library of Congress Cataloging-in-Publication Data
St. John, Jetty.
    Hispanic scientists/by Jetty St. John
    p. cm.
    Includes bibliographical references and index.
    ISBN 1-56065-360-4
    1. Scientists--Spain--Biography. 2. Engineers--Spain--Biography. I. Title.
Q141.K248 1996
509.2'2--dc20
[B]

                                                         95-50304
                                                           CIP

Photo credits
Telegraph Colour Library: 4
John O. Callihan: 6, 25
University of Puerto Rico: 8
NASA: cover, 16-20
Harvard Medical School: 32

Table of Contents

Words in **boldface** type in the text are defined
in the Glossary in the back of this book.

Chapter 1

What Is a Scientist?

Scientists are curious about the natural world. They ask many questions. They talk to other people with the same questions. All of them are looking for answers.

When scientists cannot find an answer, they make a guess. The guess is called a hypothesis. Scientists do experiments to test the hypothesis.

If an experiment works, the scientist tells other people about it. Often they write articles about the experiment for science magazines.

Australia and East Asia are in view in a photograph of Earth taken from space.

Other scientists repeat the original experiment. If everyone gets the same results, the hypothesis becomes a fact.

At Work

Scientists study birds, animals, and plants. They study the weather, stars, rocks, heat, and light. They study anything in the natural world. They often work in teams.

Scientists learn even when experiments go wrong. They never give up searching for answers.

Hispanic Scientists

The following chapters will introduce you to five Hispanic scientists. They are from different places. They decided to become scientists for different reasons. They are experts in different fields. They all enjoy being scientists and helping others through their work.

Scientists study the natural world, including the deserts of the southwest.

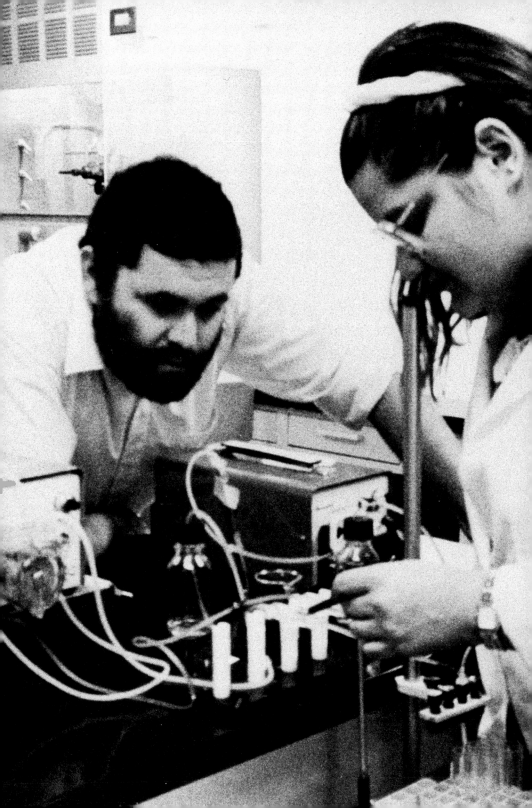

Chapter 2

Carlos A. Ramírez

Carlos Ramírez was born in 1953. He grew up in San Germán, Puerto Rico. His mother was a high-school biology teacher. She took him to class when her students were working on projects for science fairs. His family encouraged him to become a doctor, but Ramírez wanted to be an engineer.

In 1974, Ramírez earned a bachelor's degree in chemical engineering at the University of Puerto Rico in Mayagüez. He was the top

Carlos Ramírez, left, works on the artificial pancreas project with a student at the University of Puerto Rico.

student in his class. In 1979, he received a **doctorate** in chemical engineering from the Massachusetts Institute of Technology (MIT). He was the first Puerto Rican to get this degree from MIT.

Biomedical Engineering

Ramírez mixed engineering with medicine and became a biomedical engineer. They build artificial body parts. In time, it is likely that such artificial organs will be used for transplants worldwide.

When an organ in a person's body is diseased or injured, the organ sometimes needs to be replaced. The operation to replace an organ is called a transplant. Doctors use real body organs for transplants whenever they can. But real body organs for transplants are in short supply.

Biomedical engineers like Ramírez need to find materials for artificial organs that the body's **immune system** will tolerate. They also

Carlos Ramírez and his wife, Ana, relax by a lake during a vacation in Reston, Virginia.

have to design tiny medical instruments that let surgeons perform complex operations.

Ramírez is a professor of chemical engineering at the University of Puerto Rico. He is working on two major projects.

One project is the development of an artificial pancreas. The pancreas is an organ that helps the body digest food. Some people have a disorder of the pancreas called **diabetes.** Severe diabetes can lead to blindness, kidney damage, and death. An artificial pancreas could save many lives.

Ramírez's other project is the development of implants to release drugs into the body. With drugs implanted under the skin, people would not have to remember to take their medications.

The Artificial Pancreas

The pancreas produces a substance called insulin. The body needs insulin to properly use blood sugar. A person with diabetes has a pancreas that does not produce enough insulin. Many diabetics have to take daily insulin shots.

Carlos Ramírez grew up in San Germán, Puerto Rico.

Ramírez has designed a pump that works like a plastic pancreas. It is smaller than a hockey puck. It provides the body with insulin as it is needed. The outer casing is made of transparent plexiglass, a kind of plastic.

Inside the pump are cells that produce insulin. They come from a **donor** animal or person. They are protected by a thin layer of plastic called a membrane. The membrane allows the blood carrying sugar to flow in. It keeps out the blood's large immune cells that would attack the donor cells.

Help for the Body

Blood flowing out of the pump carries insulin through the patient's body. It helps the body use or store sugar.

When this artificial pancreas is ready for use in people, diabetics may no longer need daily insulin shots. The artificial pancreas has no batteries or electrical parts. It can be restocked with fresh insulin-producing cells if necessary.

A continuous supply of insulin may solve some of the problems diabetics have now.

Skin Implants

Ramírez is also working to develop skin implants that would dispense drugs throughout the body. These plastic devices slowly break down, releasing the medicine over a few months' time.

When people take pills or liquid medications, they often have to remember to take their medications every few hours. With skin implants, the release of drugs is continuous.

The implant is placed under the surface of the skin. As the drugs are released into the body, the implant disappears. It does not need to be surgically removed. Ramírez hopes to find many ways to provide medicines to people in just the right amount at just the right time.

Chapter 3

Ellen Ochoa

Ellen Ochoa became an astronaut in 1991. She was the first Hispanic woman in space.

Ochoa was born in 1958. She was a good student, and when she was 13, she won the San Diego County spelling bee. She also did well in math and science. Her discipline and dedication paid off.

She received a bachelor's degree in physics from San Diego State University in 1980. She went on to earn a master's degree in 1981 and a doctorate in 1985 from Stanford University. Both of her advanced degrees are in electrical engineering.

Ochoa's specialty is optics, which is the study of light. Ochoa's work explores how light

Astronaut Ellen Ochoa played the flute during a flight of the space shuttle Discovery.

can guide robots around objects. In space, robots perform all kinds of functions outside the spacecraft. Unlike humans, robots do not need to breathe oxygen. They can tolerate extreme temperatures and the energy from the sun called radiation.

In Outer Space

Ochoa is part of an international team of astronauts in **NASA**'s Mission to Planet Earth project. The team is trying to determine how energy from the sun changes the earth's ozone levels.

Ochoa has flown on two space shuttle missions. She performs and monitors scientific experiments. She makes adjustments to the complex instruments that measure the energy from the sun.

Measuring instruments aboard space satellites are exposed to intense radiation from the sun. Over time, this exposure makes the instruments less exact. Getting exact readings of the sun's radiation is difficult.

Ellen Ochoa flew with four other astronauts on the space shuttle Discovery in 1993.

Some of the instruments Ochoa monitors can take exact readings of the energy coming from the sun. The measurements can be used to regulate other instruments on the spacecraft. Ochoa is also trained to operate a robotic arm that releases and retrieves satellites.

Ellen Ochoa checks a camera during a shuttle flight.

The earth is protected from the sun's radiation by a layer of **ozone** gas that surrounds the planet. The **ozone layer** absorbs radiation from the sun. But scientists have discovered that the ozone layer is being damaged. To protect the ozone layer from further harm, they must discover what is causing the damage.

Ochoa and her fellow astronauts are trying to find out how many of the changes in the ozone layer are natural and how many are caused by human activities. Even small changes in the amount of the sun's radiation that reaches the earth can affect the climate. The changes can cause hot, humid conditions or cause long periods of cold weather.

Some human activities that damage the ozone layer are the burning of **fossil fuels** and the releasing of dangerous chemicals into the atmosphere. Some of these chemicals are used in refrigerators, air conditioners, and some **aerosol** sprays.

Years to Find Answer

The question of how exactly the ozone layer is affected and damaged will take a long time to answer. Scientists think that it will take nearly 100 years before the answer is known. The information available now is being shared among scientists from all over the world.

Ochoa says there is nothing she would rather do than be in space. She has a busy schedule. Still, she makes time to visit schools to encourage students, especially girls, to study hard and not be afraid of success.

Chapter 4

Eloy Rodriguez

Eloy Rodriguez was born in 1947 in Edinburg, Texas. His parents and older relatives had little formal education. Rodriguez's love of nature came from his grandfather who had a farm. From his aunts he learned about plants and how they can be used for medicines. Often, his family went for walks and collected seeds that they brought home to grow.

A school counselor suggested that Rodriguez go to a technical training school. He and his family ignored the advice. Of his 67 cousins, 64 earned bachelor's degrees. Rodriguez and four other cousins went on to

Eloy Rodriguez explores the Amazon River in South America. He studies plants from around the world.

get doctorates. Rodriguez got his bachelor's degree in zoology. He received a doctorate from the University of Texas in 1975.

Medicine From Plants

Rodriguez became a professor at the University of California in Irvine. There, he studied many plants from the Sonora Desert, which stretches from Arizona and California into Mexico. One of the plants was the strong-smelling creosote plant. In Spanish, it is called the hedionda, meaning little stinker.

The creosote contains more than 500 potential medical drugs. Native Americans of the Sonora Desert told Rodriguez that they use the plant for treating colds, stomach upsets, menstrual pains, and even dandruff.

Early Southwest Indians used a plant called brittlebush to treat mouth sores and infectious diseases. Rodriguez discovered in his travels around the world that often women are the ones who learn how to use medicinal plants. Then they pass the information on to their children.

The creosote plant and barrel cactus grow in the deserts of the southwest. The creosote has more than 500 potential medical drugs.

African Chimps

Rodriguez is now a professor at Cornell University in Ithaca, New York. One day he received a phone call from Richard Wrangham

in Africa. Wrangham was a professor of anthropology at Harvard University. He had spent 25 years studying **primates** in the wild. Wrangham told Rodriguez that wild chimpanzees in Africa had been seen picking prickly, spicy-tasting leaves with their offspring.

The chimps were carefully rolling up the leaves and swallowing them whole. Parents taught infants what kinds of leaves to pick. If the young chimps reached for the wrong plant, their parents smacked them.

These rolled-up leaves passed through the chimps' digestive systems and ended up in their droppings. Wrangham asked Rodriguez to analyze the digested leaves in the laboratory. He wanted to know what was in them.

Medicine Leaves

Rodriguez was happy to look at the leaves. One of his passions is searching the tropical

Monkeys in Costa Rica are some of the animals studied by Eloy Rodriguez.

Eloy Rodriguez is a professor at Cornell University. He established a new area of research with another professor from Harvard University.

world for natural medicines. The leaves that arrived belonged to the sunflower family.

Rodriguez looked at them under the microscope. He could see the surface of the leaf was damaged. This might mean a natural compound was released as it went through a chimp's digestive system.

Inside the leaves Rodriguez found a red oily substance that is effective against parasites, viruses, and fungi. Rodriguez thought that the chimps were probably using the leaves as a prevention or a cure for worms.

He ran more tests on the red substance. He found it could act against tumor cells. This substance might one day lead to a cure for cancer in humans.

New Area of Research

Rodriguez called Wrangham back with the news. The two scientists decided to work together. They established a new area of research called zoopharmacognosy. It is the study of plants and other natural products used by animals as medicines.

Eloy Rodriguez, in the patterned shirt at top right, posed as a child with his grandfather and cousins.

Rodriguez understands the chemistry of plants. Wrangham knows about the behavior of animals. By analyzing the plants animals eat, especially when they are sick, they hope to find new drugs that can help other animals and humans.

Chiles

Rodriguez is also interested in the nutritional value of such plants as chiles. Traditionally, in South America, Mexico, and the southwestern United States, chiles are used in many dishes.

Fresh chiles have about twice as much vitamin C as oranges. Powdered chiles are a good source of vitamin A. They reduce the risk of blood clots. They can even help the digestive system. And they are very hot. Rodriguez wants to know why.

Encouraging Others

Rodriguez works hard to share his knowledge with others. He has been recognized as one of the top 100 Hispanic educators in the country. He encourages minority children to study science. He wants them to develop critical thinking and reading skills.

Chapter 5

Lydia Villa-Komaroff

Lydia Villa-Komaroff comes from a family of six children. She was born in 1947 and grew up in Santa Fe, New Mexico.

Few of her classmates, especially the girls, studied science. Villa-Komaroff could not understand why. She went to a summer science camp. She took as many science classes as she could in high school.

In 1970, she received an honors degree in biology from Goucher College in Towson, Maryland. She continued her studies in biology at the Massachusetts Institute of Technology. In 1975, she became the third Mexican-American woman in the United States to get a doctorate in science.

Lydia Villa-Komaroff studies the brains of mice and humans at Harvard Medical School.

Young students work with Lydia Villa-Komaroff in the lab to learn what being a scientist is really like.

Villa-Komaroff is an associate professor of neurology at the Harvard Medical School in Cambridge, Massachusetts. Neurology is the study of the nervous system. She also works at the Children's Hospital in Boston.

She is studying the natural chemicals that make brain cells grow. She studies both mouse and human brains because the way their brains work is similar.

Work With Children

Her work at the Children's Hospital centers on children who have problems with the way their brains function. Some of the children suffered brain damage during birth. Others are mentally retarded because of defective genes. Some have seizures caused by brain injuries or diseases.

She hopes that by understanding normal brain development she can understand what happens when something goes wrong.

Insulin-Producing Bacteria

Villa-Komaroff worked as part of the famous Walter Gilbert team at Harvard Medical School. The team tried to develop **bacteria** that produced insulin. They took tiny pieces of **genetic material** from rats. The genetic

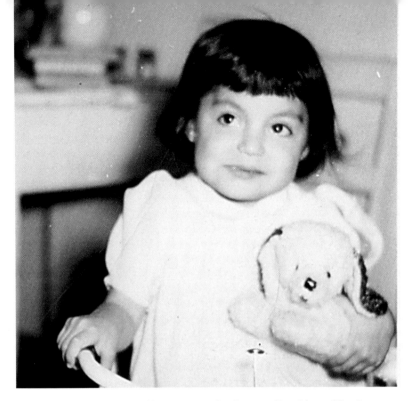

Lydia Villa-Komaroff grew up in Santa Fe, New Mexico.

material contained the instructions to make insulin. The team placed it inside bacteria.

The experiment worked. The bacteria were able to produce rat insulin. The next step was to use human genetic material to produce human insulin.

Research Banned

The Cambridge Town Council voted to ban the team's research for six months. People were worried that the scientists would produce killer bacteria. They were afraid the bacteria would escape into the environment.

At the same time, two other teams of scientists were working on human genetic research in California. Villa-Komaroff's team moved their experiments to England in 1978 where tests with human genes were allowed. After being there for only three weeks, Villa-Komaroff's husband, Anthony, called to say that one of the California teams had been successful. They had beaten her team to producing human insulin.

Dejected, her group returned home. They had not been first with successful results. They were famous, though, for their earlier work on insulin-producing bacteria. Today, millions of people suffering from diabetes receive insulin that has been produced in bacteria.

Lydia Villa-Komaroff was the third Mexican-American woman in the U.S. to receive a doctorate in science.

Helping Others

Villa-Komaroff is recognized as one of America's top scientists. She has the confidence and ability to follow her own ideas. When her research results do not turn out the way she hopes, she does not give up. She continues to look for other answers.

Villa-Komaroff remembers how few girls studied science while she was growing up. She works hard to encourage women to pursue technical careers.

She actively supports Hispanic and Native Americans in science. She has high school students work with her in her lab. There, students can learn what being a scientist is really like.

Chapter 6

Maria Elena Zavala

Maria Elena Zavala performed her first experiment with plants when she was seven years old. Her father had taken a factory job and did not need his truck to haul produce. So Maria planted lentils in it. She moved the truck between sunlight and shade as part of her experiment.

Zavala was born in 1950. She and her family lived in La Verne, California, near Los Angeles. They lived next door to Maria's great-grandmother, who was a medicine woman. She had a huge garden and used herbal medicines to cure people's ailments. Zavala learned a great deal about plants and their uses from her great-grandmother.

Maria Elena Zavala studies plants. She stands at Blue Hole, the headwater spring of the San Antonio River.

From her mother and grandmother, Zavala learned how to grow plants, bake bread, and make clothes. These skills were the foundation for her future as a successful scientist. Neither of Zavala's parents had a formal education. They encouraged Zavala and her five brothers and sisters to learn all they could at home and at school.

Zavala received a bachelor's degree from Pomona College in 1972. She earned a doctorate in botany at the University of California in Berkeley. Today, she is a biology professor at California State University in Northridge.

Plants in Cold Weather

Zavala specializes in the structure of plant roots. She is especially interested in beans and corn. She hopes to develop seedlings with roots that can tolerate cold conditions.

Farmers like to plant their crops early, when the weather is still cold. If the plants have time to develop strong root systems, they are

Maria Elena Zavala, second from right, works with her lab group at California State University.

generally stronger. Then they can survive harsh conditions. Even in sunny California, frosts can kill plants.

Passing on the Tradition

Zavala picked beans and corn to study because she likes to eat them. She grows many of her own fruits and vegetables. Just as she learned to use plants for cooking and medicines from her mother and grandmother, she hopes to pass on this knowledge to her daughter.

Glossary

aerosol—small container in which gas under pressure is used to spray liquid

bacteria—one-celled organisms that can cause diseases

diabetes—condition in which the body cannot store or convert sugar into energy, usually caused by a lack of insulin

doctorate—the highest degree awarded by a college or university

donor—person or animal that gives something from its physical self

fossil fuels—substances formed in the earth like coal, petroleum, and natural gas that are burned for energy

genetic material—the instructions inside a cell that decide specific characteristics, like the thickness of hair, which are passed from parents to offspring

immune system—part of the body that protects it from diseases

NASA—National Aeronautics and Space Administration

ozone—a poisonous form of oxygen that smells like weak chlorine

ozone layer—thin layer of ozone, 12 to 15 miles (19 to 24 kilometers) above the earth

primates—mammals with highly developed brains and hands that have thumbs, like humans, monkeys, apes, and lemurs

To Learn More

Ardley, Neil. *The Science Book of Things That Grow.* San Diego: Harcourt Brace Jovanovich, 1991.

Forsyth, Adrian. *How Monkeys Make Chocolate: Foods and Medicines From the Rainforests.* Toronto: Owl Books, 1995.

Forsyth, Adrian. *Journey Through a Tropical Jungle.* New York: Simon and Schuster, 1988.

Mabie, Margot C. J. *Bioethics & The New Medical Technology.* New York: Maxwell Macmillan, 1993.

Pirner, Connie White. *Even Little Kids Get Diabetes.* Morton Grove, Ill.: A. Whitman, 1991.

Simon, Seymour. *The Sun.* New York: Morrow, 1986.

Useful Addresses

Rain Forest Action Network
450 Sansome Street, Suite 700
San Francisco, CA 94111

**Society for the Advancement of Chicanos
and Native Americans in Science**
University of California
Sinsheimer Labs
Santa Cruz, CA 95064

Young Astronaut Council
1308 19th Street NW
Washington, DC 20036

Canadian Genetic Diseases Network
2125 East Mall, Room 348
Vancouver, BC V6T 1Z4
Canada

Index